IMAGES
of America

HELENA AND
PHILLIPS COUNTY

This photograph was taken at an annual Arkansas Delta Family Gospel Fest, an event sponsored by the Delta Cultural Center. The venue, called the Cherry Street Pavilion, is a property of the center and is the site for numerous community events, including the famous King Biscuit Blues Festival. (Courtesy of the permanent collection of the Delta Cultural Center.)

ON THE COVER: Agriculture has always played a major role in the lives of the Delta people. It has been a driving force in economic development and in day-to-day life. Before the days of mechanization, field hands picked the cotton, enduring the heat and backbreaking work. The number of tractors in the Delta doubled from 1940 to 1945. Traditionally, a person with a team of mules could plow about four acres a day; with a tractor, the Delta farmer could cover 10 times that area. (Courtesy of the permanent collection of the Delta Cultural Center.)

IMAGES
of America

HELENA AND PHILLIPS COUNTY

Bill Branch and Paula H. Oliver
on behalf of the Delta Cultural Center

ARCADIA
PUBLISHING

Published by Arcadia Publishing
Charleston, South Carolina

Library of Congress Control Number: 2012948117

For all general information, please contact Arcadia Publishing:
Telephone 843-853-2070
Fax 843-853-0044
E-mail sales@arcadiapublishing.com
For customer service and orders:
Toll-Free 1-888-313-2665

Visit us on the Internet at www.arcadiapublishing.com

To my parents for their love of Phillips County
— Paula H. Oliver

To J. Martin Jellinek for all that he does for me
— Bill Branch

CONTENTS

ACKNOWLEDGMENTS

The authors would like to thank those citizens of Helena and Phillips County who shared photographs with us to be included in this publication. The majority of the images used were taken from the permanent collection of the Delta Cultural Center. The authors would like to thank those individuals who have gifted photographs to the museum.

Special thanks go out to Ann Puckett and the *Helena World*; Doug Friedlander and the Phillips County Chamber of Commerce; V. Poindexter Fiser of the Mary Louise Demoret and Poindexter Fiser collection; Steve Johnson of the Rogerline Johnson Archives, Johnson's Studio, in Helena, Arkansas; and Carla Roy and Carrie Davidson of the Tri-County Genealogy Society in Marvell, Arkansas.

The authors would like to thank Amy Gragert, intern from Southeast Missouri State University, for her assistance in the Delta Cultural Center photograph collection and Susan Carter from the Phillips Community College for her assistance in final proofing.

Finally, this book is being published on behalf of the Delta Cultural Center, a museum of the Department of Arkansas Heritage. The authors wish to thank the staff of the museum for their support of this project.

Unless otherwise cited, all photographs used in this book are from the permanent collection of the Delta Cultural Center.

INTRODUCTION

A pictorial history of Helena and Phillips County, Arkansas, produced by the Delta Cultural Center—what a great idea! Even though the center's mission includes the entire Arkansas Delta region, its physical presence is in Helena. With this collection of photographs, you, the reader, whether resident or visitor, will see a very unique and interesting geographical area and images of persistent peoples who make up the Arkansas Delta.

A lot of history—which is an understatement—happened Helena and Phillips County. Sylvanus Phillips established the county in 1820, making it one of the earliest counties carved out the Arkansas Territory. He named a new town on the Mississippi River in honor of his daughter Helena. For almost 200 years, that prime spot at the edge of the river, with its rich alluvial soil, and the hills of Crowley's Ridge have been the backdrop for a history of agriculture, fortunes made, war, floods, an intermingling of humans of all backgrounds and economic levels, and a life experience that produces a culture and music that is known worldwide.

Helena, Arkansas, is a river town—it always has been—and today the Mississippi River influences it still. Mark Twain called it "one of the prettiest situations on the river." The Mississippi is the gateway for agriculture products to ship out and for diverse peoples to move in. Phillips County, right before the Civil War, was one of the top cotton-producing counties in Arkansas. An 1860 state census table shows Phillips County with 6,022 whites and a slave population of 8,817. For this reason, Helena and the county played a large role in the Civil War in Arkansas.

Helena was the home to seven Confederate generals: Patrick Cleburne, Thomas Hindman, James Tappan, Daniel Govan, Lucius Polk, Charles Adams, and Arch Dobbins. The Union army captured Helena in 1862. It was a strategic stronghold on the river and proved its worth for the North and a disaster for the Confederacy on July 4, 1863, as the South attempted to retrieve it in battle on the same day that Vicksburg fell to General Grant.

The river's flow is ever present as it rises and falls behind the levee wall. The people and communities of Phillips County also rise and fall. Cotton production was successful even after the war with the sharecropping system. Railroads were introduced, and lumber production increased. Helena was a booming town at the turn of the 20th century with merchants and stores of all kinds on Cherry Street. Meanwhile, one block over on Walnut Street, a new American music genre called "the blues" was thriving, eventually making Helena "the blues capital of the Delta" from about 1920 to 1950. African Americans, with names such as Sonny Boy Williamson, Robert Lockwood, and Howlin' Wolf Burnett, got their start on the radio program *King Biscuit Time* on station KFFA. This music program started in 1941 and is still broadcast today from the Delta Cultural Center.

By the 1980s, agricultural production was becoming increasingly efficient, and factory work that in the past required hundreds of man-hours could now be done in a short amount of time by large machines. As with most Delta towns, there was a mass exodus of the population as people went elsewhere to look for jobs. Helena and towns like Marvell and Elaine were no exception to the flight. Many attempts have been made to revitalize life in Phillips County. A real success for Helena is the King Biscuit Blues Festival held each year in October. Literally thousands and thousands of music fans attend the event.

The people of Helena and Phillips County maintain pride in their Delta heritage and look forward to a rebirth of their towns with tourism, culture, and music events. And as the river flows by Helena and Phillips County, a surge of the spirit of hope in this place looks to the 21st century.

Enjoy this photographic trip through history. See how the river and the land have been good and bad during the years. The images in the book are only a small selection and are dependent on the collection of the Delta Cultural Center and the generosity of those who graciously shared photographs with us. May this effort pique your interest to learn more.

One

EARLY HISTORY

Published in New York by Harper & Brothers, *Harper's Weekly* featured foreign and domestic news, fiction, essays, humor, and illustrations. The political magazine was published from 1857 to 1916, and issues of the 19th century are among the more popular due to the wood engravings that documented much of American history from 1857 to the end of the 19th century. This is an example of one of the engravings and shows Helena during the 1860s.

When European explorers first set foot in the Delta, the region already had been home to Native Americans for thousands of years. By 8500 BC, northeastern Arkansas had an active population skilled in hunting, fishing, and gathering as well as other basics needed to survive in the natural world. (Courtesy of University of Arkansas Museum.)

Old Town Lake in southern Phillips County is a 1,200-acre Mississippi River oxbow lake. These *U*-shaped lakes form when a section of the river is cut off and are named after part of a yoke for oxen.

The Catholic Knights of America placed this statue of Fr. Père Marquette in 1936. In 1673, Father Marquette, a Jesuit priest, and Louis Joliet, a French fur trader, set out from Canada searching for a route to the Pacific Ocean. They started their journey at Lake Michigan, traveled down the Wisconsin River to the Mississippi River, and continued southward beyond the mouth of the Arkansas River. They are credited with discovering that the Mississippi River flowed into the Gulf of Mexico, not the Pacific Ocean.

In 1541, Hernando de Soto crossed the Mississippi River near Friar's Point, Mississippi, to Azuixo, an Indian village south of Helena. The Native Americans here were friendly toward de Soto and his men. Having never seen a white man before, the Indians thought de Soto was a god and asked him to bring rain for their scorched crops. He explained that he was not a god but that he would set up a cross in their village and hold a service, asking God for rain. This is believed to be the first Christian service west of the Mississippi River.

Estevan Hall was built in 1826 by Fleetwood and Millander Hanks and remained in the Hanks family until 1996. The family moved to Iowa during the Civil War, and Union forces occupied the house. It is currently under restoration to bring it back to its 1920s appearance, so it is very different from what is seen this photograph. (Courtesy of the *Helena World*.)

Helena was filled with beautiful homes in its early years. This row of homes is typical and shows some of the impressive architecture of the area. The styles of architecture range from Queen Anne Victorian to Craftsman. Several antebellum homes still stand today, including Estevan Hall, Moore-Hornor House, and the Tappan-Pillow house. (Courtesy of Hornor collection, Dana Kurts.)

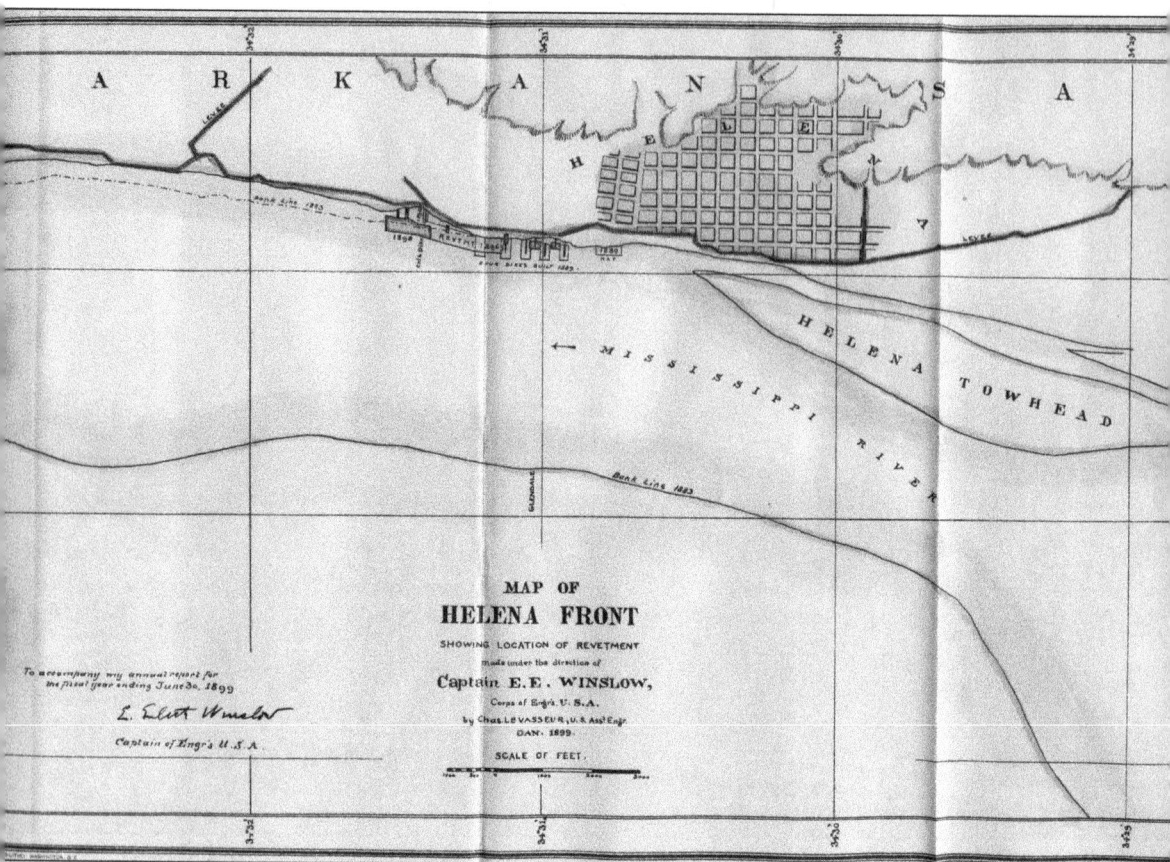

MAP OF
HELENA FRONT
SHOWING LOCATION OF REVETMENT
made under the direction of
Captain E.E. WINSLOW,
Corps of Eng'rs. U.S.A.
by Chas. LE VASSEUR, U.S. Ass't Eng'r.
JAN. 1899.

SCALE OF FEET.

To accompany my annual report for
the fiscal year ending June 30, 1899

L. Eliot Winslow

Captain of Engr's U.S.A.

The US Army Corps of Engineers consisted of a chief engineer and two assistants when it was organized by the Continental Congress in 1775. Throughout the 19th century, the work of the corps consisted of supervising the construction of coastal fortifications and mapping much of the American West. This map of Helena was created by the corps in 1899.

The Almer Home, just south of this building, was constructed in Iowa about 1870 and was floated down the Mississippi River to Helena on a barge. Some of the material in the barge was used to construct this building, known as the Almer Store. A unique feature is that the sidewalls are of post-and-plank construction with two-inch planks inset into grooves in the post.

These photographs show downtown Helena in 1895; above is Ohio Street, and below is Cherry Street. On Ohio Street, one can see Summers & Watson Hardware store on the left and a liquor store on the right. The photograph of Cherry Street was taken from the corner of Cherry and Elm Streets. The building on the right sits where the Solomon Building (Helena National Bank) was later constructed. (Both courtesy of the Hornor collection, Dana Kurts.)

In the early 1900s, Helena had all the conveniences and luxuries of a modern, state-of-the-art city. It was well lighted, both by electricity and gas, and merchants, manufacturers, bankers, and professional men were prospering. This postcard shows Cherry Street at the time when streetcars were still in operation; however, the automobile was becoming more popular.

FERN HILL CUT, HELENA, ARK.

The founders of West Helena, Edward Chaffin Hornor and John Sidney Hornor, realized the importance of connecting Helena and West Helena and thus purchased the Helena Street and Interurban Railroad Company in October 1909. They secured the right-of-way, cut through the hills, and then went on to build a streetcar line to West Helena. This right-of-way is now Highway 49, the major thoroughfare through town.

The Yazoo & Mississippi Valley Railroad (Y&MV) was incorporated east of the Mississippi River, with Helena being the only portion in 1904 west of the Mississippi. The railroad kept freight rates lower than those normally collected west of the river for eastbound freight. The Y&MV depot, shown here in 1917, was an impressive building on Cherry Street but was torn down to make way for a parking lot for the bank across the street.

Cherry Street was booming in the 1930s, with lots of retail shops, restaurants, and services. C.E. Mayer Company, a clothing store, and Truemper Furniture Company are on the left, with a gas station on the right. C.E. Mayer founded his store in 1921, stocking clothes for men and women. Joe Truemper opened his furniture store in 1893 and became so successful that he built another store on Cherry Street for his sons, thus creating competition for himself.

As early as 1808, a traveler reported seeing cotton fields north of Helena, though no cotton gins. Eleven years later, a traveler found a Delta settlement with two gins and more cotton fields along the way. This picture was taken during the 1920s or 1930s.

Two

THE RIVER

The Mississippi River is what defines the Delta region of eastern Arkansas. It was a major factor in the development of Helena as it became a hub for transportation and a significant river port. The river has shown her destructive power over the years; from 1858 to 1937, a total of 11 damaging floods struck the Mississippi River Valley.

In the decades after the Civil War, several fleets of steamboats formed on the lower Mississippi River. The Anchor Line was one of the best-known, although not very successful, steamboat companies. It operated a fleet from St. Louis to New Orleans between 1859 and 1898. The design of the Anchor Line's boats changed in 1880, when all newly built vessels were side-wheelers with two paddle wheels on either side. This design had proven to be easier to maneuver and faster than the older stern-wheelers with the paddle wheel at the rear of the boat.

Two stern-wheelers are shown in this 1927 photograph, with the *Margaret* on the right. There is high water under the storage building on the left. These steamboats were used to save the lives of people during the flood that year by transferring them and their possessions across the Mississippi River to safer places.

The *Pelican* ferry transported railcars between Lula, Mississippi, and Helena, Arkansas. The *Pelican*, Illinois Central's only service to Arkansas, was discontinued in the 1960s when a trestle leading to the ferry in Mississippi burned down. The fire appeared to be arson, leading to speculation that the railroad was somehow involved, as the fire gave the railroad an excuse to abandon the service.

Before the Helena/Mississippi Bridge was built, this ferry seen above transported automobiles and railroad cars across the Mississippi River. Completed in 1961, the Helena/Mississippi Bridge made travel between Mississippi and Arkansas easier and boosted Helena's economy by eliminating the need for ferryboats.

The *Delta Queen* first began service in California in 1927 and was considered one of the most lavish and expensive stern-wheelers ever commissioned, along with her sister, the *Delta King*. In 1946, the *Delta Queen* was purchased by the Greene Line of Cincinnati, Ohio, and began serving the Mississippi River and its tributaries. It was designated as a US National Historic Landmark in 1989. This photograph was taken during a visit to Helena in the 1980s. She no longer travels the rivers, as she was docked in June 2009 in Chattanooga, Tennessee, and converted into a hotel.

Occasionally in winter, the cold weather would cause the Mississippi River to turn into ice. In this photograph, the paddleboat *Curly* has run aground and is surrounded by frozen river water; note that the main river channel appears as though it is still flowing.

In this photograph, the mighty Mississippi River has turned into ice. A man is standing beside a mound of ice piled along the shoreline that appears to be at least 20 feet in height. These ice chunks could have been gathered to help clear the river for traffic.

The flood of 1927 was devastating to the communities in the Delta. Here is a transfer steamer crossing the Mississippi River, relocating residents and transferring property to safety. River traffic could continue during a flood's high water levels. In an attempt to hold the mighty river back, sandbags have been placed along the shoreline.

Just a year before the 1927 flood, the Mississippi River Commission had enough levees built that its members proclaimed an "end of the flood control fight along Mississippi River." Locals are shown sandbagging the Mississippi River in Elaine, Arkansas, during the flood of 1927. (Courtesy of the Mary Louise Demoret and Poindexter Fiser collection.)

This scene in downtown Elaine was typical of small towns hit hard by the flood of 1927. The streets were entirely flooded, and water ran into the buildings. Residents fled to higher ground, but some may have stayed to watch over their property.

The lumber mills at Wabash suffered from flooding in the late 1920s. Railroad boxcars were turned into makeshift living quarters for refugees in this lumber mill yard. Note the laundry hanging on the line (on the left, at the end of the first set boxcars). (Courtesy of the Mary Louise Demoret and Poindexter Fiser collection.)

The river is rising in this scene from Helena during the 1920s. The mighty Mississippi River looms ominously in the background. Some neighborhoods of Helena are on higher ground, but the majority of the first downtown buildings have always been susceptible to flooding. Here, work continues as smoke rises from a smokestack.

The steamboat *Capitol* is shown moored at the banks of Helena during the flood of 1927. This steamboat could have come into the harbor to avoid the high water out in the main channel of the river, or it could be close as a means of transporting passengers either upriver or downriver. Note the high water on the limbs of nearby trees.

By May 1927, the amount of acres of tillable and uncultivated land under water totaled 4,149,500. When the Mississippi River floods, all of the rivers in the United States that flow into it also flood. The result is that the water in the tributaries cannot flow into the main channel, thus tributary rivers actually flow backwards and flood the lands around them.

As of May 1, 1927, the *Arkansas Democrat* newspaper estimated flooding in Arkansas had then already affected 30 counties, killing 78 people and inundating 1,376,000 acres of farmland. In this photograph, groups of people are walking out to a sandbagged deck to be rescued by an approaching steamer. (Below, courtesy of the Mary Louise Demoret and Poindexter Fiser collection.)

An estimated 84,600 people were displaced, 22,095 head of livestock drowned, and 6,478 houses were swept away during the flood of 1927. Above, all that is left of a sharecropper's house has been flipped by the water, and to the right a man in hip boots is wading in what was once a street.

In March 1927, the National Weather Bureau in Memphis warned of record-breaking floods as the river in Memphis exceeded the 10-foot flood stage. Over 13 inches of rain fell there, and floodwaters soon began 111 consecutive days lapping at Helena's levee. The people the boat seen above include Catherine Reid, Dorothy Reid, Charleen Reid, and Jack Reid.

With floodwaters having nowhere to go, much of Arkansas remained under water through the spring and summer and into September 1927. Farmers could not plant crops, and the carcasses of thousands of dead animals lay rotting in stagnant pools. The conditions were perfect for mosquitoes, increasing the threat of disease.

The Red Cross raised over $17 million for flood relief. Although their lives were interrupted, normal activities still took place. These photographs show refugees eating dinner at the railroad terminal in downtown Helena and participating in Sunday services at the camps. Below, note the organist and choir in the pickup truck from a West Helena store.

The American Red Cross responded quickly to the disaster, with emergency workers arriving by trains, trucks, and automobiles. Fifty refugee camps were set up around the state similar to the one in the photograph above. The homeless found themselves without food, water, or dry clothing. Refugees did have opportunities for medical help, as shown in the photograph below; pictured are people waiting to enter the "Doctor Tent."

The 1928 Flood Control Act authorized the Mississippi River and tributaries project. Carried out by the Mississippi River Commission, the project employed a variety of engineering techniques, including an extensive levee system to prevent disastrous floods in the future. This photograph shows a levee being built in Helena in 1929.

Three

CIVIL WAR

During the Civil War, there was no time to construct forts in the traditional manner, so all fortifications, on both sides, were constructed with earth. Fort Curtis, named after Union general Samuel Curtis, was built by US Army troops and paid contraband labor. It was an earthen defensive position to secure Helena as a supply link for Union operations in Arkansas and the Vicksburg campaign. (Courtesy of Library of Congress.)

The Tappan-Pillow House was built in 1858 and was once the home of James C. Tappan, one of seven Confederate generals from Helena. Tappan was serving in Little Rock at the time of the Union occupation of Helena, and like others in town, his home was confiscated by Union troops. Tappan survived the war, returning with his wife to Helena and resuming his law practice and political career. (Courtesy of the Kappi Pillow collection, Jerry Pillow.)

The Union army confiscated the Robert Caswell Moore home to serve as Gen. Frederick Salomon's headquarters. Graveyard Hill, the site of the bloodiest confrontation during the battle, is located directly behind the house. Two holes in one of the parlor doors are attributed to shots fired through a back window. The house was donated by the family to the Delta Cultural Center in 1995 to be used in the interpretation of the Civil War in Helena.

The homes of prominent Confederates were often confiscated by Union troops. Such was the case with the home of Thomas C. Hindman, commander of Confederate forces in Arkansas. The taking of this home by Gen. Samuel R. Curtis for his headquarters was a personal statement on the Union victory symbolized by the occupation of Helena.

The Confederate Cemetery in Helena contains the graves of many of the Southern casualties of the Battle of Helena, which took place on the Fourth of July in 1863, as well as the final resting place of one of the South's great generals, Helena resident Patrick Cleburne. The Confederate Monument pictured here is a granite shaft with a life-size statue of a Confederate soldier done in Italian marble at the top; the whole column stands 37 feet high. It serves as a memorial for the Confederate dead who fell at Helena and other engagements in eastern Arkansas.

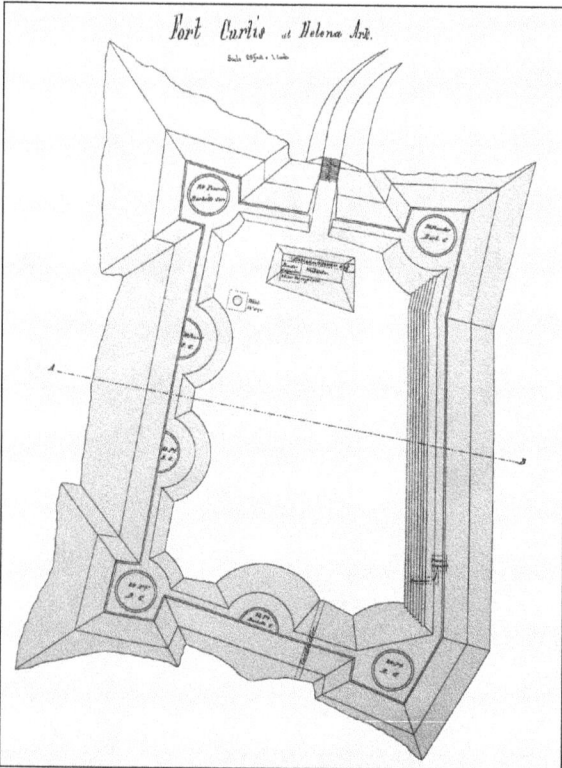

At left is a detailed drawing of the original Fort Curtis submitted by Capt. William Hoelcke, chief engineer of the Army of the Southwest. Below is a photograph of a replica of Fort Curtis, completed in 2012, located two blocks from the original site. It is three-fourths the size of the original. (Left, courtesy of National Archives; below, Paula H. Oliver.)

Born and raised in Ireland, Patrick Ronayne Cleburne became the most popular Confederate division commander and was known as the "Stonewall of the West." After immigrating to the United States in 1849, Cleburne settled in Helena and worked as a pharmacist. He later became a wealthy lawyer. He joined the Confederacy and began his meteoric military career, developing a reputation as one of the finest infantry commanders in the South. Cleburne reached the rank of major general and died in the Battle of Franklin. His body was originally buried in Franklin, Tennessee, but his remains were later moved to Helena, Arkansas.

The Confederate States of America suffered many kinds of shortages during the Civil War, the hardest being the lack of a sound currency. The man responsible for Confederate finance was Secretary of State Christopher G. Memminger. He made the disastrous mistake of issuing paper money unsupported by gold. Individual states and local towns also printed currency. This action caused rampant inflation in the Confederate states. By the end of 1864, the value of a Confederate dollar dropped to nearly zero. Shown here is a fragment of a bill printed in Phillips County.

In July 1862, the Union army marched into Helena, capturing the city. Helena was occupied for four years by Union troops, most coming from the Midwest. Pictured above is the 29th Iowa Camp at Helena in 1863. Seen below is the 9th Wisconsin Infantry boarding steamboats in Helena in 1864.

During the Civil War, St. John's Episcopal Church was located at the southwest corner of Cherry and Rightor Streets. It can be seen in the background, to the left of the boat, in this image of a flood.

Conditions were harsh, with soldiers and residents having to endure disease, extreme heat, and floods. As a result of crowded conditions, hot weather, and poor sanitation, many men became sick and hundreds died. The 19th-century understanding of disease and sanitation was part of the problem; many of the drugs given to soldiers were actually poison, including mercury and silver nitrate. Helena became "Hell in Arkansas" to many Union soldiers.

When Gen. Samuel Curtis crossed the state of Arkansas to reach Helena, he allowed fugitive slaves to follow his army along the way. Considering them as contraband of war, he offered protection from their former owners and their first taste of freedom. During the war, thousands of slaves sought refuge in Helena, with hundreds joining the US Army in the federally occupied city. This camp was just south of town.

Four

COMMUNITY
DEVELOPMENT

Agriculture has been the primary industry in Phillips County. Cotton was "king" for years, and this photograph shows the Helena Cotton Compress Company in its heyday. Note the pressed bales of cotton, the railroad tracks, and the excess cotton on the ground. In order to improve shipping and save money, cotton was compressed into packages called bales.

The men in the photograph give good perspective of the size of this cypress tree. The image was taken in Elaine in the early 1900s. Forests of cypress swamps have vanished from the Delta. Cypress is a hardwood that lasts a long time. (Courtesy of the Mary Louise Demoret and Poindexter Fiser collection.)

Lumber mills were plentiful in Phillips County. These men worked for Howe Lumber Company in Wabash during the 1930s. The workers are sitting and standing at the base of inclined railroad tracks that would allow a lumber train to push cars of logs into the mill. (Courtesy of the Mary Louise Demoret and Poindexter Fiser collection.)

Both of these photographs are of Howe Lumber Company in Wabash. The image above shows lumber being transported by both mule-drawn wagon and by train, while the one below depicts "Lumber Alley." Lumber mills were able to industrialize the making of planks used in building construction. Huge logs came into the mills and left as uniform wooden planks ready for builders.

Trees were abundant and large, as these photographs taken in Elaine during the 1920s and 1930s show. Various methods were used to transport the logs to the mills. The forests of Phillips County yielded much wood, and the lumber was shipped all over the country. (Both courtesy of the Mary Louise Demoret and Poindexter Fiser collection.)

Another industry was this hoop plant in Elaine, where hoops for wooden barrels were made. The hoops held the curved wooden planks that made up a barrel. Barrels were very sturdy and the most common container for shipping or storage. (Courtesy of the Mary Louise Demoret and Poindexter Fiser collection.)

Chicago Mill and Lumber Company was located in West Helena and employed hundreds of workers in its heyday. It was one of the largest wood processing industries in West Helena during its boom years. This is a portion of a panoramic photograph taken during the 1920s. (Courtesy of James Mathis and Donald R. Mathis.)

During the time that cotton was the predominant crop, scenes like these were common, with wagons lining up to ship it out in the early 1900s. The images depict the Marvell area. Compressed cotton bales were transported to towns or cities back East via train or steamboat. (Both courtesy of Edwynne Hirsch Storey.)

In this c. 1910 photograph of Marvell, bales of cotton are stacked on railcars to be shipped to other parts of the country. Marvell, even though smaller than Helena, produced its share of cotton to export. Phillips County still yields cotton today, harvested in modern ways. (Courtesy of Edwynne Hirsch Storey.)

Workers take a break at the cotton plantation of Lily Peter in western Phillips County. In addition to being a successful farmer, Lily was a philanthropist and poet. Piled high behind the workers are truckloads of hay, which was important in feeding mules and other livestock.

Before the days of mechanization, cotton was picked by hand and collected in these long tow sacks. Here, in 1931, sacks are being weighed in Marvell. When cotton was harvested by hand, it was collected in large burlap sacks that pickers pulled. Many of the workers may have been hired for just the day, and after each one, sacks were weighed and wages paid according to weight. (Courtesy of Tri-County Genealogy Society.)

Opening *NEW HORIZONS*

FOR INDUSTRY ... FOR COMMERCE ... FOR A BETTER WAY OF LIFE

Dedication Day Program – July 27, 1961

HELENA · WEST HELENA, ARKANSAS

July 27, 1961, was a very important day in the growth of Helena and West Helena. Three sites were dedicated: the Helena Bridge, an industrial plant, and the Federal Building. This is the cover of the Dedication Day Program. Many residents of Phillips County felt that they had entered the modern age with these improvements and that much progress would be coming their way.

The new Arkansas Power and Light Company Ritchie Steam Generating Plant provided new jobs to Helena in the 1960s. The new power plant sits on the shores of the Mississippi River and provides electricity for the eastern region of the state of Arkansas. (Courtesy of Phillips County Chamber of Commerce.)

In the forefront is the *Spirit of the American Doughboy* statue, a tribute to the men and women of Phillips County who served in World War I. The statue depicts a typical soldier, rifle in hand, as he goes "over the top" of a hill hurling a hand grenade before him. The statue was dedicated in July 1927 and was a project of the Phillips County Memorial Association. Helena's city hall is seen as it was during the 1950s. This building was replaced in the late 1960s with a larger, more modern building. (Courtesy of David Henson Sr.)

Helena and West Helena were proud to see the new Helena Hospital built, situated between the two towns atop Crowley's Ridge. Not only was it a major employer, it provided needed medical care that enhanced the quality of life. A new hospital was later built on the bypass around town, and the old hospital was converted into apartments.

The Phillips County Port Authority had the ground-breaking ceremony for the new Slack Water Harbor in 1989 with several dignitaries present, including then-governor Bill Clinton, Sens. David Pryor and Dale Bumpers, and Rep. Bill Alexander. It consists of 4,000 acres of flood-protected industrial sites centered on a 2.25-mile, nine-foot-deep slack water channel. The site is located six miles south of Helena on Highway 20. (Courtesy of Phillips County Port Authority.)

60

In 1886, the Helena Electric Light and Power Company was organized and constructed an electric lighting plant. Constant improvements in the business soon revealed the need for a larger plant. The Helena Gas Company purchased the electric plant and consolidated it with its gas business. (Courtesy of Phillips County Chamber of Commerce.)

This aerial shot of Helena was taken looking south and includes the area from Beech Street east to the river. Note that there is no bridge, so the photograph was probably taken in the 1940s or 1950s. The building on the right with the large parking lot was a grocery store at the corner of Pecan and Porter Streets. Just below that are the Methodist and Episcopal churches.

The development of West Helena was the result of efforts by two cousins, Edward Chaffin Hornor and John Sidney Hornor. In 1907, they began to realize the limitations for the growth of Helena. They began to look to the west side of Crowley's Ridge for economic development. In 1910, a survey and map of the new town showed an extraordinary plan. Lots were laid out to certain requirements, 10-acre industrial sites were laid out along the railroad, and many other zoning requirements were specified. This photograph of West Helena was taken in the 1960s. (Courtesy of the *Helena World*.)

Local law-enforcement officers pose for the camera around 1933. From left to right are chief deputy E.P. Hickey, assistant prosecuting attorney John Anderson, and Sheriff F.F. "Happy" Kitchens. Hickey later became sheriff and served for 20 years. Hickey's son Marion S. Hickey followed him as sheriff, also serving for 20 years. (Courtesy of the Hickey family.)

Using an old 1934 model bus that had belonged
to Brocato Bus Line, Marvell's first fire truck
was crafted by Sib Davison at Erwin Motor
Company. The "red light" on the front of the
truck was created by pouring Mercurochrome
on the clear lens. Since most able-bodied
men were off fighting in World War II, high
school students were automatically dismissed
from school to fight fires when they occurred.
(Courtesy of Tri-County Genealogy Society.)

Downtown Helena had plenty of restaurants
in the 1920s and 1930s. In 1937, there were
nine restaurants in downtown Helena, as well
as saloons and pool halls. Pictured here is the
Bell Café, located at 101 Missouri Street in the
Garofas Building. Many residents remember
this as Nick's or Casqui's Restaurant.

Downtown Helena had an abundance of retail shops that sold everything from clothing to jewelry to hardware. The King family owned both of shops seen here. Pictured above is the King Family Store, located in the Solomon building, and below is King Men's Ware Store, located at 310 Cherry Street. (Both courtesy of John King Jr.)

Mom-and-pop businesses were scattered all over Phillips County, providing a variety of products and services. The Padula Grocery Store at 1248 Holly Street was typical of small grocery stores in the 1930s. Pictured are Frank Padula and Anna Cordi Padula in the 1930s. (Courtesy of Mary Ann Taylor.)

The sponsor of the *King Biscuit Time* radio show, Interstate Grocery Company began marketing Sonny Boy Cornmeal in order to capitalize on the popularity of Sonny Boy Williamson, who became the show's most famous performer. Sonny Boy was known for his ability on the harmonica and inventive songwriting skills and is acknowledged as one of the most influential blues musicians.

INTERSTATE

Grocery Company

(In Business Since 1913)

We Recommend-

KING BISCUIT FLOUR

THE ALL PURPOSE FLOUR

One of the South's Finest

Let us include a few barrels in your next order

THANK YOU

Montgomery Ward was another example of the plentiful retail in downtown Helena. In 1872, Aaron Montgomery Ward founded the company. It began as a mail-order business but expanded to retail outlets in 1926. From the 1950s to the 1990s, it struggled to adjust to increased competition and the movement of the middle class to suburbia. The company filed for bankruptcy in 1997 and closed for good in May 2001.

Customers of Interstate Grocery Store could keep track of items they wanted to purchase in this "Want Book" from the 1950s. Max Moore owned the store. He agreed to be the original sponsor of *King Biscuit Time* radio show after being approached by Sonny Boy Williamson and Robert Lockwood Jr.

Rogerline Johnson was a photographer best known for his images of African American life in the Arkansas Delta in the 1950s and 1960s. Pictured is the original office of Johnson's Photo Shop, at the corner of Arkansas and Biscoe Streets, in the 1950s. The name was later changed to Johnson's Studio, and the business was relocated a few blocks north. (Courtesy of Rogerline Johnson's Archive, Johnson's Studio, Helena, Arkansas.)

West Hornor Motor Company has been a prominent business in downtown Helena since 1924. The dealership is seen here in 1956. It started out on Walnut Street but moved to this location on the 600 block of Cherry Street after a couple of years. The next move would be just a couple of blocks away to its current location on Perry Street. (Courtesy of the *Helena World*.)

Louise and G.W. Russell, proprietors of the Halfway House, are shown in 1966. The Halfway House was a local favorite and was one of only two restaurants that offered curbside service at that time. It was located halfway between Helena and Helena Crossing, hence the name. (Courtesy of the *Helena World.*)

Another longtime business in downtown West Helena is Plaza Barbershop, established in 1946. Pictured are customers Louis Grobmyer (left) and Ashley Higgins receiving haircuts from barbers Skeet Seaton (left) and Dale Ishmael. The shop is still in business today in spite of competition from numerous beauty salons that have attracted more business from the male population. (Courtesy of Skeet Seaton.)

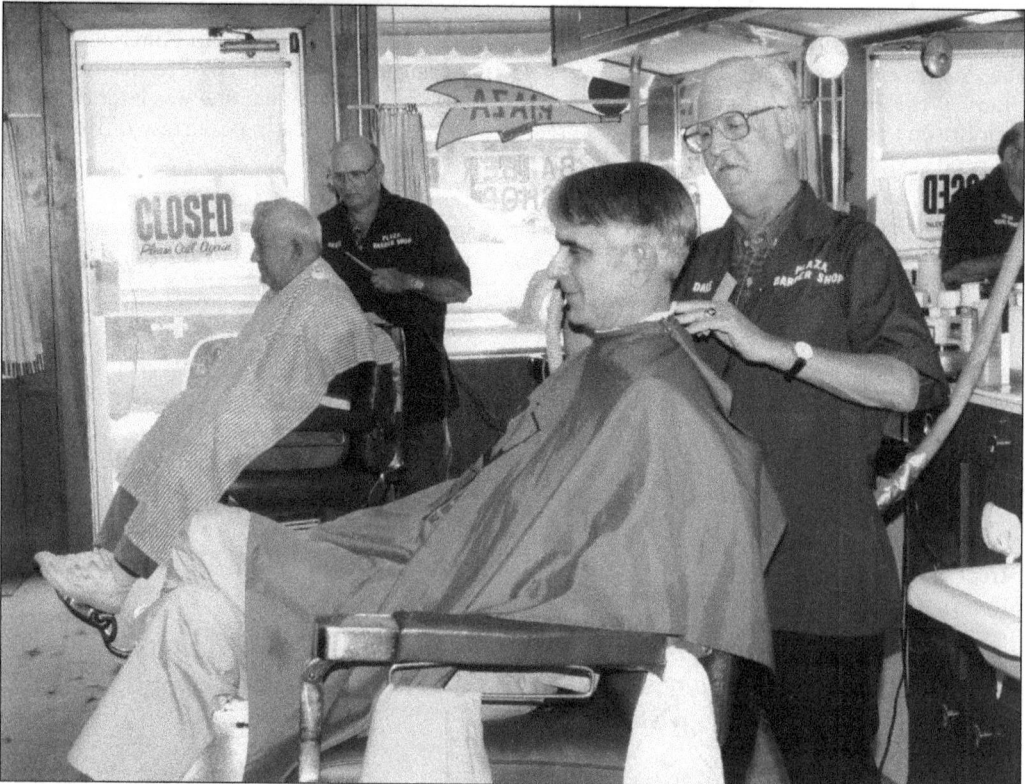

Downtowns in smaller communities like Elaine were bustling during the 1930s, with a variety of shops and services available on Main Street, including this clothing store. Having such a variety provided local citizens with products and kept them from having to shop in the "city" of Helena. (Both courtesy of the Mary Louise Demoret and Poindexter Fiser collection.)

The Bank of Elaine was organized in 1919 but closed after the 1927 flood. Note the ornate teller's cage and the marble floor. Delta State Bank opened for business in 1948 with William O. Demoret as president. Today, it is part of Southern Bancorp. (Courtesy of the Mary Louise Demoret and Poindexter Fiser collection.)

Pictured in the 1930s or 1940s, the Connor Taylor Liquor Store was located on Main Street in Marvell. It was the original building for A. Hirsch & Company, which did a tremendous mercantile business. The liquor store was unusual because it served food as well as selling alcohol. Local residents remember a sign on the outside that read, "Hamburgers, 5 cents." (Courtesy of Tri-County Genealogical Society.)

Bass Grocery Store in Postelle and the Marvell Auction Company are good examples of successful small businesses. Postelle is a small community located west of Marvell close to the county line. Businesses have flourished in Marvell since it was established. In the early 1900s, there were 15 different merchants in the city. (Above, courtesy of the *Helena World*; below, Tri-County Genealogical Society.)

While Marvell's economy has always been based on agriculture, small downtown businesses provided needed services and products. This is downtown Marvell during the 1920s. On the left is the Bank of Marvell, which closed in 1972 when a new bank was built on Highway 49. The old bank building is still standing. (Courtesy of Tri-County Genealogical Society.)

Harry Kelley acquired land around what is now Elaine in 1892. He came to Elaine and began clearing the land and selling timber. Kelley was responsible for building the first railroad, and W.M. Allen came to Elaine to manage the first depot. Pictured are locomotives at the Elaine depot sometime in the 1920s or 1930s. (Courtesy of the Mary Louise Demoret and Poindexter Fiser collection.)

In 1944, Missouri Pacific (MoPac) had five passenger trains going in and out of Helena from Brinkley, Clarendon, Wynne, and Memphis. The demand was so great that MoPac created a special train, the *Delta Eagle*, which was unique in that it was a dedicated express commuter to Helena. On May 14, 1941, the *Delta Eagle*, an engine with two cars, was introduced to Arkansas.

The Farm Security Administration established Lake View as a resettlement project to help relieve rural poverty. The community was built in an area where farm labor problems were especially severe. Incorporated in 1972, it is located on the banks of beautiful Old Town Lake. Here, folks wait at the depot in Lake View sometime in the 1920s or 1930s. (Courtesy of the Mary Louise Demoret and Poindexter Fiser collection.)

AeroTech was a flying school located just outside of West Helena in the 1940s. Helena had been selected over three other sites, and the city made a number of key concessions in securing the facility, which provided considerable employment and income for the area. Instruction was given in the techniques of military flying as opposed to civilian flying. The students came out of a civilian pilot training program, which screened potential pilots before coming to Helena. The program consisted of 10 weeks of primary flying, and each training group had about 200 men. In all, some 3,985 students pilots graduated the program at AeroTech.

Five

ARTS AND CULTURE

Arts and culture have enhanced the lives of Phillips Countians for decades, providing music, art, museums, dramatic productions, and cultural celebrations. Whether the talent was homegrown or a visiting artist, the citizens of this county have benefitted from exposure to a wide range of experiences, including touring opera and dance companies and nationally known performers.

Parades and civic celebrations were very popular during the early years. These events added excitement to the lives of ordinary people. Seen here is prominent Helena resident John Sidney Hornor II (in robe in front, sixth from the left) as king of Mardi Gras. He seems to have arrived in Helena via the Mississippi River in the company of his court.

Flower parades were common and included horse- and mule-drawn buggies, as well as early automobiles. Local flowers were picked from gardens and then attached to the vehicles to make a "float" similar to today's Rose Parade in Pasadena, California. In the carriage are Robert Hornor and Carolyn Hornor; on the pony is Bess Straub; horse attendants are Ben Bailey (left) and Cleve Clements (right).

Elaborately decorated cars were part of this parade in Helena during the 1920s; flowers cover every part of these vehicles. Ladies and gentlemen from Helena wore their very best clothes for parades, crowds gathered along the streets to view the flowers, and parasols were opened to protect delicate skin from the sun.

Marvell had its share of parades. This horse and buggy seem to be waiting for a parade to start. Before the day of the automobile, this was the customary mode of transportation. Other than horse-drawn vehicles or riding a horse, people walked to their destination. (Courtesy of the *Helena World*.)

This mule-drawn hay wagon was part of a parade down Plaza Street in West Helena during the 1950s. The parade was more than likely commemorating an anniversary, and people were remembering times past. Mules played an important part in agricultural production; they were the "power" that today comes from machines.

The Helena Shrine Club participated in an event, probably a parade, in Jonesboro, Arkansas, in the 1920s. The Helena club was a part of Sahara Shrine Temple in Pine Bluff, Arkansas. In this photograph, there are initiates and a clown unit. The organization is an advanced level of Freemasonry and takes its themes from Arab and Asian heritage.

Organized groups such as the Masons were present in many towns. Pictured is the Masonic lodge in Marvell. The Freemasons are a fraternity of men whose origins are debated but take their symbolism from the ancient craft of stonemasonry. Their buildings are usually two stories with the meeting room on the top floor. (Courtesy of Tri-County Genealogy Society.)

Built by the Clem Brothers for Charles Lawson Moore, this structure has served as a courthouse, a Presbyterian church during the Depression, and a cadet club during World War II. It most recently has operated as a bed-and-breakfast inn. Typical of many of the great old homes in Helena, it has large rooms, a wraparound porch, and a turret.

An annual fair and livestock show emphasized the importance of agriculture to the local economy and showed the work of farmers. This is the cover of a program for the 1947 Farmer's Community Fair and Livestock Show in Marvell. Over the years, it grew to become the Tri-County Fair, including Phillips, Lee, and Monroe Counties.

Helena children Marguerite Hornor and Roy Grimes, both six years old, are shown participating in a Tom Thumb wedding. The real General Tom Thumb was a little person who became an entertainer with the Ringling Bros. Barnum & Bailey Circus and, in a highly publicized and opulent wedding, married in 1863. Americans revered the event, and a humorous play based on the spectacle was performed by community ensembles all over the country. The play evolved into scripted mock weddings featuring children, called "Tom Thumb weddings," which were fundraisers for schools and churches.

The former Missouri Pacific depot in Helena was restored in the late 1980s and opened in 1990 as the Delta Cultural Center, a museum of the Department of Arkansas Heritage. The museum preserves a permanent collection on Delta heritage. The "Heritage of Determination" exhibit traces the history of man's efforts to live and prosper in the Arkansas Delta.

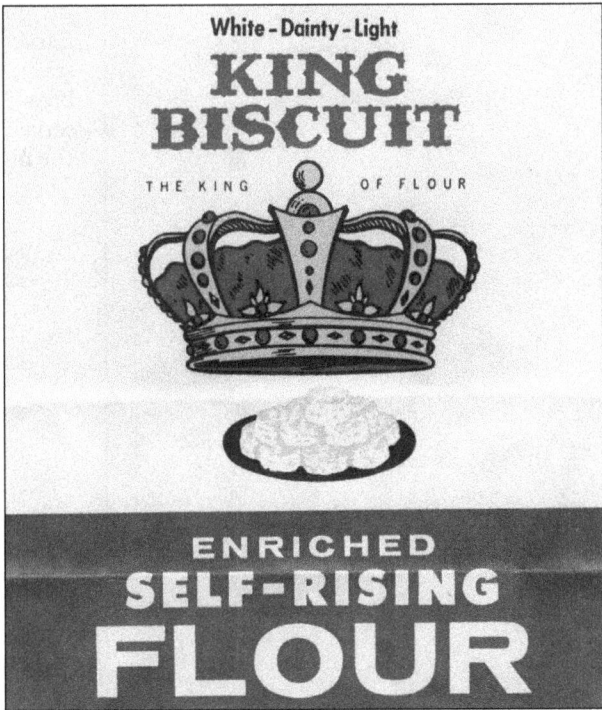

King Biscuit Flour has become a highly recognizable name due to its connection to the *King Biscuit Time* radio show and the world-renowned King Biscuit Blues Festival. It was a product of the Interstate Grocer Company, which sponsored the original radio show, *King Biscuit Time*. Slogans for the flour were "The King of Flour" and "White-Dainty-Light."

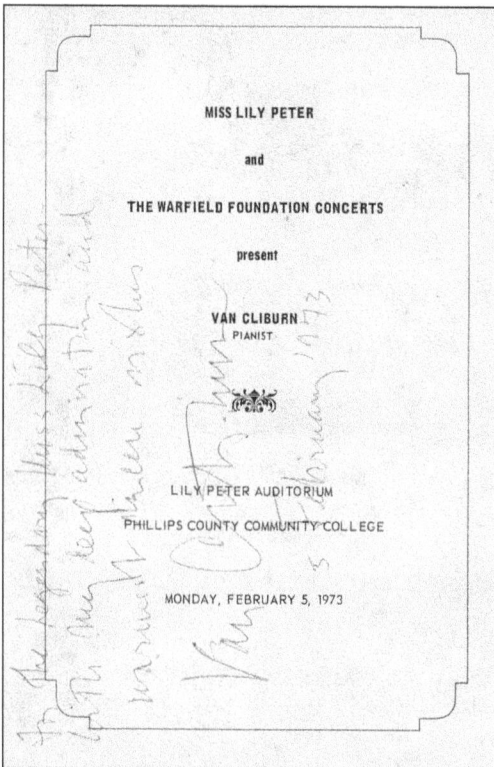

Philanthropist Lily Peter and pianist Van Cliburn are shown having a light supper after his Warfield Concert performance in 1973. Earlier in the evening, before he went on stage, he dined on turnip greens and corn bread, which he had requested; they were served with a big juicy steak! Also shown is the program cover autographed by Cliburn.

This original charcoal drawing shows the impressive talent of Helena artist Dewitt W. Jordan Jr. He formally studied art while attending Tennessee State University. He then moved to California and worked for Warner Brothers Studio as a backdrop painter. Upon returning to the Delta in the 1960s, Dewitt set up studio space above the family funeral home and spent nights meeting musicians in juke joints around Helena. These musicians were often the subjects of his paintings. Dewitt's cousin, Fred M. Jordan III, recalled that Dewitt loved African American people deeply and anguished over their struggle, often painting "dirt under their fingernails or cavities in their teeth."

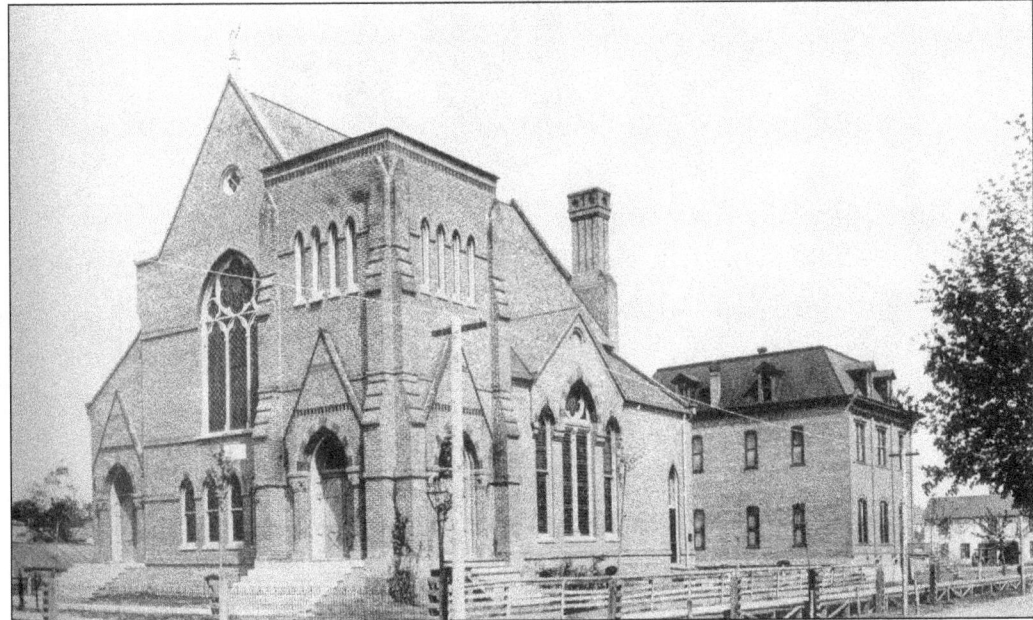

Pictured is the former First United Methodist Church. Behind it to the right is the Phillips County Library, which opened its doors to the public in 1891, making it the oldest public building in the county. The first collection of books given the title "library" dates back to 1874. This photograph was taken in 1895. (Courtesy of the Hornor collection, Dana Kurts.)

"Sunshine" Sonny Payne began working as a paperboy in 1940 and became friends with blues musicians Sonny Boy Williamson and Robert Lockwood Jr. He began working at radio station KFFA in 1941 as a janitor and errand boy. In 1942, in the absence of the station's owner and announcer Sam Anderson, he began reading commercials on the station's 15-minute slot sponsored by the King Biscuit Flour Company; he also began learning to play bass. Later that year, he joined the US Army. He left the armed forces in 1948 and began working as a bass player, touring with Tex Ritter, Harry James, and others until 1951. Payne then returned to Helena and secured a job as an announcer at KFFA, working as presenter of *King Biscuit Time*. His show is reportedly the longest running daily show in radio history and is internationally recognized. It is currently broadcast from the KFFA studio located in the Delta Cultural Center in Helena.

Helena's first local radio station, KFFA 1360 AM, went on the air in November 1941. Soon after, owner Sam Anderson was contacted by blues musicians Robert Lockwood Jr. and Sonny Boy Williamson with a pitch to air a local blues radio show. Anderson thought the idea had promise and directed the musicians to Max Moore, owner of Interstate Grocer Company, as a possible sponsor for the show. Hoping to appeal to an African American market, Moore agreed to sponsor the show if the men would endorse his product. With Moore on board, the *King Biscuit Time* radio show went on the air on November 21. From left to right are Sonny Boy Williamson, Sam Anderson, and Robert Lockwood Jr.

Roger Johnson & His Orchestra were "tops in dance music" and toured several Southern states during the 1950s and 1960s. Roger Johnson (far right) later started Johnson's Studio and was a well-respected Helena photographer. The studio is still in operation and is run by Roger Johnson's son Steve Johnson.

Helena-born saxophonist and clarinetist Red Holloway had a career that spanned over 60 years. He performed with a variety of artists, including Billie Holiday, Lionel Hampton, Bobby Bland, and B.B. King. During the last years of his life, he performed jazz, primarily as a solo artist. He died in February 2012 at age 84.

A former resident of Marianna, rockabilly singer Jimmy Evans was a member of the Arkansas Jamboree for eight years. Evans's career spans 40 years, and he currently resides in Helena. His recordings "The Joint's Really Jumpin'," "Messy Bessie," "Dudley Do-Rite," and "Pink Cadillac" are considered rockabilly classics, earning him induction into the Rockabilly Hall of Fame.

An American electric blues musician, guitarist, singer, and songwriter, Michael Burks is shown donating his guitar to the Delta Cultural Center in 2005. Burks played in Helena many times before passing away unexpectedly in 2012. He is best known for his tracks "I Smell Smoke" and "Hard Come and Easy Go."

The town of Elaine in south Phillips County played host to Sparkman, Arkansas, native and well-known American country music star "Jim Ed" Brown, who performed with his sisters as The Browns. The band's best-known track is "The Three Bells." (Courtesy of the Mary Louise Demoret and Poindexter Fiser collection.)

Sam Myers was an American blues musician and songwriter, with a career that spanned decades. He performed as the featured vocalist for Anson Funderburgh and the Rockets at the King Biscuit Blues Festival in Helena many times before his death in 2006. He is shown here at the first King Biscuit Blues Festival in 1986. (Craig Baird, photographer.)

Bill Branch, curator for the Delta Cultural Center, is also a talented watercolorist. This is a painting he did in 2012 of the Delta Cultural Center's Visitor's Center on Cherry Street during a street fair called Helena Second Saturdays. This building has temporary exhibit galleries, offices, and the Delta Sounds Room. (Courtesy of Bill Branch.)

The Helena Country Club was the site of many social activities in Helena and West Helena. Dances were very popular, and members enjoyed golf, swimming, and dining, as well as occasional special events. This building burned in 1969 and was replaced with a newer structure on the far side of the golf course.

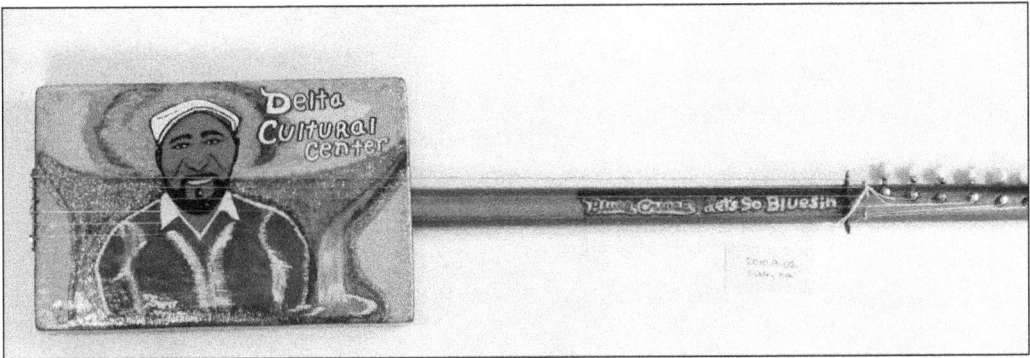

A diddley bow is a handmade guitar-like instrument with six strings that has a wooden sound box with a neck. This instrument was personalized for the Delta Cultural Center by James "Super Chikan" Johnson in 2010 and has a self-portrait of the artist on the front of the instrument.

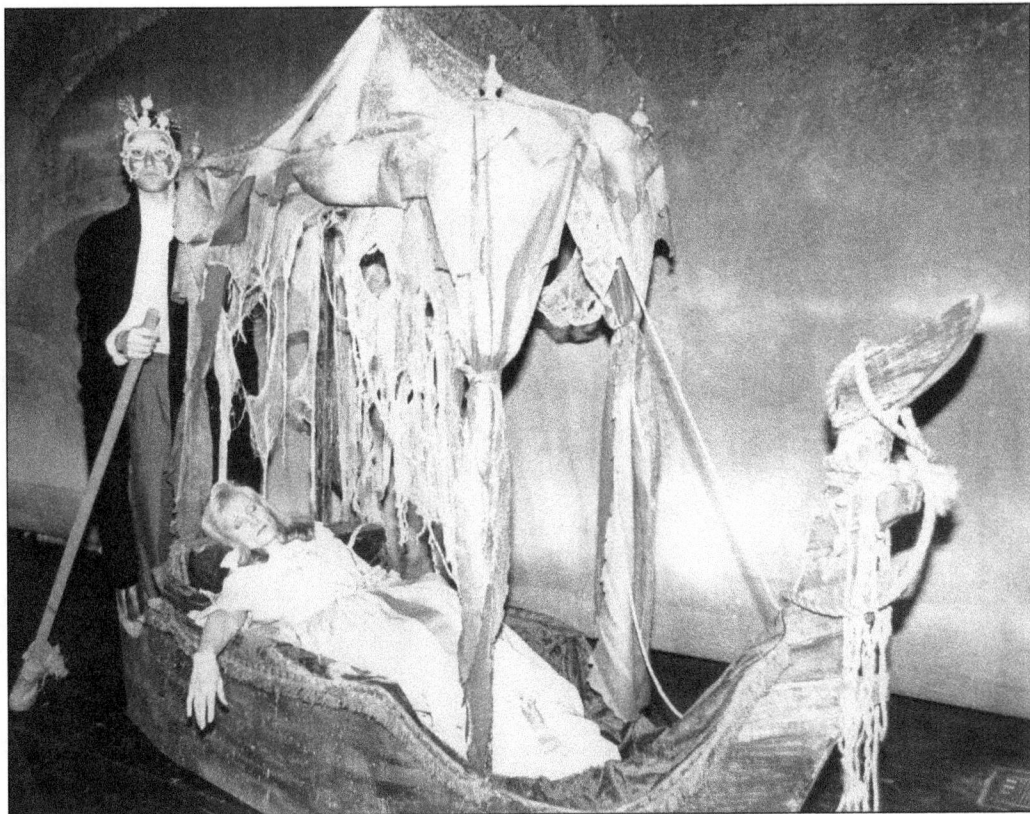

Helena Little Theatre is one of the oldest nonprofit organizations in Phillips County. Over the last 78 years, it has presented musical theater and dramatic productions using local talent. This photograph is from the production of *Phantom*. The productions are staged at the local community college. (Courtesy of Helena Little Theatre.)

Each year, the King Biscuit Blues Festival, sponsored by the Sonny Boy Blues Society, has an art competition to produce the winning poster for that year's festival. This is the acrylic painting *Homecoming* by artist Cristen Craven Bernard. It was the 26th-annual King Biscuit Blues Festival poster winner.

Six

Religious Life

CORDER CHAPEL

In the South, it seems like there is a church on every corner—big or little, country or urban, organized or nondenominational. Religion has always been an important part of the lives of the people of Phillips County. Churches provide a place to pray, to praise, to sing, and to enjoy fellowship.

This photograph of New Light Missionary Baptist Church shows its 1917 church building designed in free interpretation of the Gothic Revival style. This building was razed in 2006 to make room for a new building for this predominately African American congregation. The new structure occupies the exact same space in Helena.

The congregation of New Light Missionary Baptist Church is celebrating the pastor's anniversary in this 1950s photograph. The pastor and his wife are pictured with the clothes they wore on their wedding day. In case her assistance is needed, a registered nurse is seated by the door. (Courtesy of Rogerline Johnson's Archive, Johnson's Studio, Helena, Arkansas.)

Built in 1916, Temple Beth El became home to a growing and vibrant Jewish congregation that formed in 1867. Many of the Jewish families that settled in Helena played important roles in developing the area, with success in business and civic affairs. After reaching a peak of 400 members in 1927, membership began to decline during the second half of the 20th century, along with Helena's population and economy. With only 20 members in 2006, the temple was donated to the State of Arkansas for use by the Delta Cultural Center as Beth El Heritage Hall.

Bishop John Maury Allin was born in Helena and was ordained an Episcopal priest in 1945. In 1974, he was elected to serve as the 23rd presiding bishop of the Episcopal Church. Bishop Allin was chosen to lead the church during one of its most divisive periods, as various factions were starting to press for the inclusion of African Americans and women. He retired as presiding bishop in 1985 and died in 1998. (Courtesy of St. John's Episcopal Church.)

The first Episcopal service held in Arkansas took place in Helena in 1839. St. John's Parish was founded in November 1853 and has had three buildings. Taken by Rev. Frank G. Walters, rector from 1936 to 1944, this photograph shows the sanctuary of St. John's Episcopal Church about 1940. The church was completed in 1915 and still stands today at the corner of Perry and Pecan Streets. (Courtesy of St. John's Episcopal Church.)

St. John's Episcopal Church in Helena had a large girls' choir that provided special music during the year. This photograph was taken during the mid-1940s. The occasion must be Easter Sunday, as the church is decorated with lilies. The church's priest is on the far the left, and the male cross and candle bearers are in the back center. All of the girls' heads are covered with caps, as was the custom of the day.

Dedicated in 1936, St. Mary's Catholic Church (above) was the fulfillment of a lifelong dream of Fr. Thomas J. Martin. Three relatively unknown young men were chosen to build this work of art, and all of them went on to reach national fame in their respective fields: the architect was Charles Eames, who made a name for himself in modern furniture and architecture; Emil Frei installed the stained glass and was considered one of the world's finest window designers; and the mural on the sanctuary wall was painted by Charles Quest, whose works are in permanent collections all over the world. The first Catholic church in Helena dates back to a small brick building (right) in 1856. (Both courtesy of the Don Eastman collection.)

Church records show that the Rev. Benjamin Burrows was preaching in Helena as early as 1822. A year or two later, a society of Methodists was organized by local preachers who filled the pulpit until 1830. At that point, the church was made a part of a circuit and supplied with regular pastors and presiding elders. In 1848, Helena was made a station. The church organization was

suspended during the Civil War, with nothing in church records except "war, war, war." Around 1925, the board of the local church hired Lucy E. Critz as director of religious education, and the church flourished. This photograph was taken on Mother's Day in 1922. (Courtesy of Helena First United Methodist Church.)

The Methodist congregation has had a regular place of worship in Helena as early as 1840. The first church was destroyed before the Civil War, and the congregation relocated to a building somewhere on Cherry Street. That structure was sold in 1860, and the congregation decided to build on the site of the present church, which was a gift from John Sidney Hornor. The church was completed in 1885 but was partially destroyed by fire in 1913. The church was rebuilt and still serves an active congregation. This photograph shows the church during the 1940s. (Courtesy of Helena First United Methodist Church.)

What is now known as the First Baptist Church of Helena was first organized in 1852 with about a dozen charter members. The first home of this church was the old courthouse that stood on the corner of Perry and Franklin Streets where a prominent evangelist conducted services. The first house of worship was built in 1854. This photograph shows the church as it is today.

Here is the second building used by the First Presbyterian Church, located on the corner of Franklin and Porter Streets. This building was later sold to the Christian Church when the Presbyterian congregation built a new church at the corner of Porter and Columbia Streets. (Courtesy of Helena First Presbyterian Church.)

The Elaine Methodist Church is shown here in the 1930s or 1940s. The building features a bell tower, and the lower portion is a brick structure while the upper portion has a wood shingle finish. There are screens over the windows to allow for open windows in the days before air-conditioning. (Courtesy of the Mary Louise Demoret and Poindexter Fiser collection.)

The Elaine Methodist Church had an active youth choir, shown here in the 1940s. Fresh young faces of these children show excitement at the taking of this photograph. They are dressed in their cassocks and surplices, and the adult leaders stand in the back right. (Courtesy of the Mary Louise Demoret and Poindexter Fiser collection.)

The Baptist Church of Elaine had a sizeable congregation in the 1940s when this photograph was taken. The impressive brick building was designed in a Greek Revival style, and the main auditorium area is located on the second floor. This feature of having the main assembly area higher off the ground is common to churches in Phillips County for flooding reasons. (Courtesy of the Mary Louise Demoret and Poindexter Fiser collection.)

Centennial Baptist Church was designed by African American architect Henry James Price and built in 1905. One of the early ministers was Dr. Elias Camp Morris, who was born a slave in Georgia but moved to Helena in 1877 and became an important state and national religious leader. One of his most notable accomplishments was his presidency of the National Baptist Convention, the largest denomination of black Christians in the United States. Dr. Morris died in 1920 and is buried in the Dixon Cemetery. The church was designated as a National Historic Landmark in 2003.

The Marvell Baptist Church displays beautifully arched stain-glass windows. The brick building is designed in Gothic style with towers. Again, the main auditorium in this building is located on the second floor because of the possibility of flooding. Sunday school rooms and a reception area are located partially below ground level. (Courtesy of Tri-County Genealogy Society.)

Part of congregation of the Corder Chapel is seen here in 1951. A mixture of adults and children pose in their "Sunday go to church" clothes. The small wood-frame building has a tar-paper covering to resemble bricks. The chapel was located on Perry Street Extended. (Courtesy of the *Helena World*.)

Trenton Baptist Church is a good example of a country church. The small brick building is adorned with a steeple on the roof. The smaller extension at the back would be for education rooms. The metal tank to the far left is for storing fuel to heat the building. The church is located in the Poplar Grove community in the western part of Phillips County. (Courtesy of Tri-County Genealogy Society.)

Seven

EDUCATION

This iconic building was constructed in 1914 and symbolizes the importance of education to the people of Phillips County. It originally served as the high school for Helena, but it became the elementary school when a new high school was built to accommodate students from both Helena and West Helena. In 2012, a renovation project began to convert the school into apartments.

Southland College grew out of the Freedmen's Asylum for Orphans, an orphanage and school founded in 1864 by the Indiana Yearly Meeting of Friends (Quakers). Originally called Southland School, it operated as a boarding school, offering a secondary education to African American students from throughout the South. After adding a teacher training curriculum, the name was changed to Southland College. Its educational mission continued into the first quarter of the 20th century. (Courtesy of the Special Collections, University of Arkansas Library, Fayetteville.)

From an insignificant wooden building with two or three teachers in 1889, public schools in Helena grew to employ a dozen teachers at Jefferson School alone and accommodated 400 students. Built in 1895, Jefferson was an impressive structure that stood on the west side of Pecan Street between Porter and Rightor Streets until it was razed. (Courtesy of the Hornor collection, Dana Kurts.)

The students from Marvell Public Schools are shown here during the 1920s. Two significant events took place in the 1960s that affected the educational system of the town. In 1966, Marvell Academy, a private school, was formed, and in 1967 Marvell Public School became fully integrated. (Courtesy of Tri-County Genealogy Society.)

Elaine's first school was built in 1915 and graduated five students in 1924. The building most likely housed the entire student body of Elaine Public Schools. It unfortunately burned in 1925 and was replaced with one in a different location. (Courtesy of the Mary Louise Demoret and Poindexter Fiser collection.)

Many high school fraternities and sororities founded in the 19th and 20th centuries in the United States grew into national organizations with highly evolved governing structures and regularly chartered chapters in multiple regions. Many of the local chapters were not tied to, or affiliated with, individual high schools. They were often regional, drawing membership from multiple high schools in a given area. Helena had two high school fraternities, Delta Sigma and Sigma Phi Omega, and one sorority, Delta Beta Sigma. Here, members of the Delta Sigma fraternity are shown on a trip to California in 1924. From left to right are James King, Baxter King, Clancy King, and Robert Handley. (Courtesy of John King Jr.)

Helena and West Helena each had a high school until 1949. At that time, students from both towns attended the newly built Central High School that sits between Helena and West Helena. This is the 1927 senior class of Woodruff High School in West Helena. (Courtesy of the *Helena World*.)

Phillips Countians have always loved sports and supported their high school teams with enthusiasm. Pictured is the Elaine High School football team in 1928. During this time, football jerseys were made of thick, heavy material, oftentimes wool. This was also the time when wearing helmets was optional, as can be seen in the image. (Courtesy of the Mary Louise Demoret and Poindexter Fiser collection.)

The Helena High School class of 1932 is seen here on the front steps of the school. Note the small children looking on in the background by the awning. The heavy coats indicate that it is fall or winter, and all the women have on skirts or dresses—no pants.

Jerome Pillow practices for a Helena High School track meet in the 1930s. The group in the background appears to be a combination of parents, teachers, and fellow students and track team members. The young man third from the right appears to have a camera. (Courtesy of the Kappi Pillow collection, Jerry Pillow.)

This 1937 Elaine High School football team looks ready to hit the gridiron. Note the leather helmets some players are wearing, which were not mandatory during games until the 1930s.

Both of these photographs are from Marvell schools. The photograph above shows what is likely the entire student body at the time, and below is the basketball team in the late 1940s. Note the uniforms as they compare with uniforms of more recent years. (Both courtesy of Tri-County Genealogy Society.)

Originally the home of Col. Henry L. Biscoe, this property was purchased by the Catholic Church in 1858 and opened as St. Catherine's Academy, a convent and day school operated by the Sisters of Mercy. During the Civil War, the school was used as a hospital for the blue and the gray. In 1879, the school reopened as Sacred Heart Academy and continued to operate until lack of funds caused its closing in 1968. The building was sold to the Helena Housing Authority and finally demolished in the early 1970s. (Courtesy of the *Helena World*.)

Mattye Maye Woodridge spent her life as an educator, working as a teacher and administrator for four decades. The first Teachers' Day that Woodridge put on was a local celebration at Eliza Miller School in 1944. These events continued until 1953 under her supervision. During that time, she began a campaign to gather support for a National Teachers' Day, contacting political and education leaders on the state and national level. Woodridge credited former first lady Eleanor Roosevelt as the prime mover in persuading the 81st Congress to pass a joint resolution in 1953 designating the first Tuesday in March as National Teachers' Day. (Courtesy of Rogerline Johnson's Archive, Johnson's Studio, Helena, Arkansas.)

Cheerleading was an activity that involved both male and female students. Here are the Central High School cheerleaders in front of the gymnasium sometime in the 1950s. From left to right are Pat Gladin, Marjorie McGee, Shirley Umfress, Walter Vernon Dunivant, Evelyn Griffin, Sherytha Payne, and Janice Spears. (Courtesy of the *Helena World*.)

High school students also participated in sports outside of campus. Pictured are members of the 1960 Helena Mohawks, Arkansas American Legion state champions. From left to right are (first row) Captain Dwight Galloway (manager), Milton Alexander, Blake Robertson, Charlie Williams, Mike Brady, Joe Ed Darnell, Tommy Galloway, Shea Bearden, and coach Gene Bearden; (second row) Ladner "Laddie" Crouch, Richard Sands, Carter Enlow, Ken Harfield, Bill Gray, Bob Heslep, Earl "Butch" Wilson, and Jimmy Schaffhauser; in front is Sheriff Marion Hickey (the commissioner). (Courtesy of the Hickey family.)

The campus of Central High School served students from both Helena and West Helena. The long building on the right housed the ninth and tenth grades, while the upperclassmen attended "up the hill." The gymnasium is the building closest to the football field. Students are walking around the dirt track during a physical education class. (Courtesy of the *Helena World*.)

In 1925, Eliza Miller, the wife of a successful African American businessman in the Helena area, bought and donated land to the local school district for a high school to be built to serve the African American students in the area. Showing off new uniforms, the Eliza Miller High School band is marching in a parade down Missouri Street in downtown Helena during the 1960s. (Courtesy of Rogerline Johnson's Archive, Johnson's Studio, Helena, Arkansas.)

Charleen Reid Hickey was a teacher at Central High School in Helena for 30 years. Originally from Elaine, she taught a variety of subjects, but Spanish was her passion. In recognition of her dedication to teaching and devotion to her students, she was named Arkansas Teacher of the Year in 1968, the only Phillips County teacher to achieve this honor. (Courtesy of the Hickey family.)

Established in 1965, Phillips County Community College was one of the first community colleges in the state of Arkansas. This photograph shows the first few buildings of the campus, constructed on the hills of Crowley's Ridge. In March 1996, residents of Arkansas County passed a referendum to annex the county into the PCCC taxing district. The name was changed to Phillips Community College to reflect the multicounty support, and plans began to expand the off-campus programs in Stuttgart and Dewitt. On July 1, 1996, Phillips became a member of the University of Arkansas System.

Lily Peter Auditorium in the Fine Arts Center on the campus of Phillips Community College has hosted many events, including Warfield Concerts, dance recitals, graduations, and dramatic productions. This 1,100-seat auditorium was completed in 1973 and has excellent acoustics, an orchestra pit, and a full-time technical director. Pictured are Lily Peter, who led the fundraising efforts to build the Fine Arts Center, and pianist Van Cliburn as he prepares for a Warfield Concert performance in 1973.

ABOUT THE DELTA CULTURAL CENTER

The Delta Cultural Center in historic downtown Helena preserves, interprets, and presents the heritage of the 27-county region of eastern Arkansas that makes up the state's portion of the Mississippi River Alluvial Plain. The center provides a foundation from which many tales of the Arkansas Delta can be told.

Central to our mission are three museum properties open to the public: the Visitor's Center at 141 Cherry Street; the restored 1912 Missouri Pacific depot, a block away; and a replica of the Union army's Fort Curtis at 350 Columbia Street. The Delta Cultural Center also has two other historic properties that are open on an as-needed basis: the 1859 Moore-Hornor House at 323 Beech Street and the Beth El Heritage Hall at the corner of Pecan and Perry Streets.

The Delta Cultural Center Depot, located south of the Visitor's Center, presents our acclaimed permanent collection on Delta heritage and exhibits on the Civil War Battle of Helena. At the Visitor's Center, one can catch a live daily broadcast of *King Biscuit Time*, the nation's longest-running blues radio program; Delta Sounds, a permanent exhibit that provides a look at the variety of musicians and musical genres of the Arkansas Delta; and changing exhibits of art, history, and culture. The Fort Curtis replica offers a self-guided tour of the earthen fortification constructed during the Union occupation of Helena during the Civil War.

The Delta Cultural Center offers lectures, programs, seminars, musical festivals, performances, and other cultural offerings throughout the year. Please check our website for the most current offerings and news at www.deltaculturalcenter.com.

Visit us at
arcadiapublishing.com

www.ingramcontent.com/pod-product-compliance
Lightning Source LLC
Chambersburg PA
CBHW050631110426
42813CB00007B/1782